The Know Your Neuro series is dedicated to kids everywhere who are busy growing, strengthening and protecting their brain.

This book, Neuro Feels Feelings, is dedicated to Mary Clara, a girl who has learned how to listen to and understand her feels.

Library of Congress Cataloging-in-Publication Data
Collier, Crystal.
Neuro Feels Feelings (K-2)
1. Substance use-Prevention 2. Youth-Drug Use 3. Education-Juvenile
Literature 4. High-risk behavior-Risky behavior

ISBN 979-8-9896642-0-7

NEURO FEELS FEELINGS

By:
Crystal Collier, PhD, LPC-S

Illustrated by:
Rachel Joanna

Just like a true superhero,
Neuro is growing and going on lots of
adventures...

To discover how the brain learns
new things and makes good choices!

Because the brain is a very important body part!

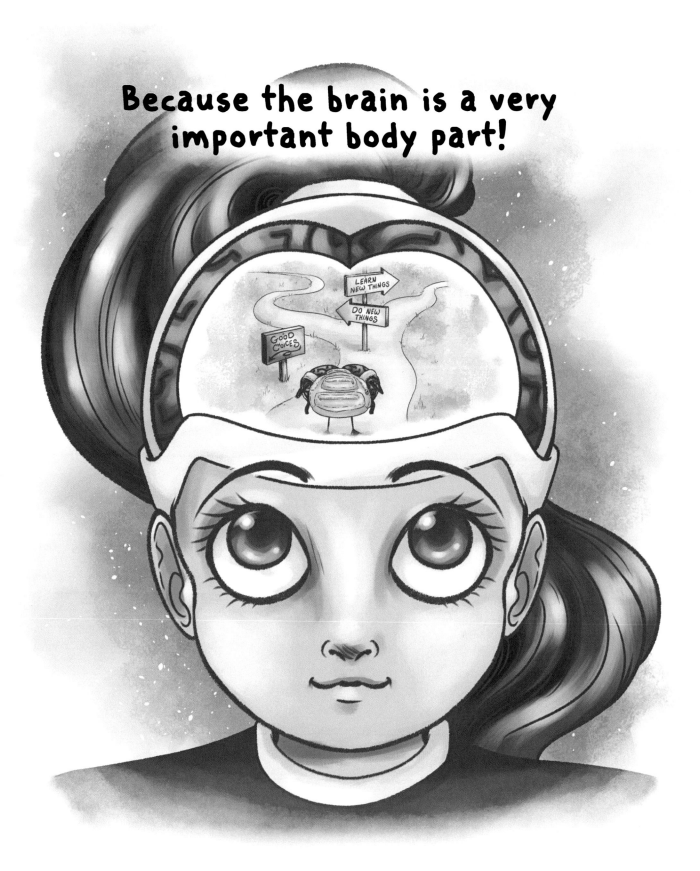

Everything you think...

...feel...

...and do...

...happens
in the brain.

That's why
Neuro is a superhero!

Neuro learned to follow
the Brain's rule 'Use it or Lose it'
and practice making good choices
because using that thinking skill
builds good judgment.

Good judgment is knowing
what is good and not so good for you.
Good judgment helps keep you
and Neuro safe.

Neuro is ready
for another exciting adventure!
What does Neuro want
to learn about next?
How to name and understand
feelings!

Feelings can be confusing
and hard to understand.

Wow!
What an adventure!
Neuro is determined to find out what feelings are and what to do with them!

What are feelings?

Feelings are sensations in the body that are telling you something. Neuro must figure out what they are called and what they mean.

You might notice your feelings causing sensations in your heart or in your stomach.

Sometimes, you can feel sensations all over your skin, from the top of your head to the tip of your toes!

Some feelings are warm and calming.

Other feelings may make it seem like there are butterflies in your tummy.

And other feelings may make your heartbeat faster.

Your brain helps you name what the feeling is called and understand what it means.
Feelings give us information!

Feelings tell us what we need
or what we want.
That is why it is important to practice
naming and understanding your
feelings.

Wow! Naming and understanding feelings seems like it could be hard or even confusing!

How will Neuro do it?

First, Neuro notices
the sensations in the body that signal
we are having a feeling.
Then, Neuro figures out what the
feeling is called.

There may be times when you don't know the name of the feeling that you are feeling!

That's ok! Ask for help!
A trusted adult like a parent or teacher might know. Or you could use a feeling face chart.

Next, Neuro tries to figure out
what that feeling means.
What is the feeling trying to tell us?

What does the body need or want?

Neuro feels a warm, fluffy feeling
in the body's heart.

This feeling feels good!
What does that sensation mean?

What is the name of that feeling? It's

Does that feeling mean that you want to smile?

Or laugh?

Or hug someone?

Whoa!
Now Neuro feels tightness
in the body's chest and notices
the hands are making fists!

What is that feeling
and what does it mean?

Yes!

That is

Anger tells the body it needs to pause, take a few slow, deep breaths and calm down.

Here comes
another uncomfortable feeling.
Neuro notices a tingling in the tummy.
Does this mean you are scared or sad
and want to talk to an adult?

Does it mean you need to stop eating something yucky because you feel disgusted?

Or does it mean you need to ask for help with something because you feel worried?

There are no right or wrong feelings.
Whatever you feel is okay!
Even if another person tells you that
you should not feel that way,
your feelings are special
and an important part of
who you are!

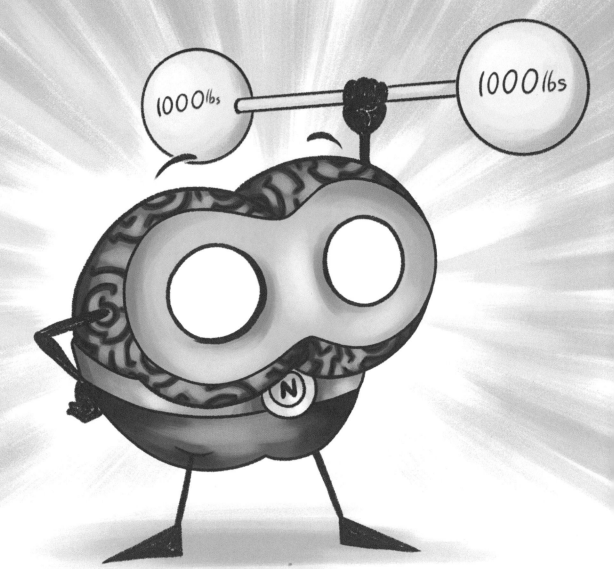

Wow!
Listening to and understanding
your feelings can be hard!
Neuro knows that practicing this skill
will help keep your brain strong.
How will you practice recognizing
and learning from your feelings
to keep your brain strong?

Let's practice this skill like Neuro!

Think of 3 feelings you have. Name them and describe what you need or want when you feel them?

1. When I feel _____,
I need or want _____.

2. When I feel _____,
I need or want _____.

3. When I feel _____,
I need or want _____.

Wow! You are getting really good at this skill!

Fill out the My Strong Brain Pledge!

Ask for help cutting it out of the book.

Hang it on the wall where you can see it to remind you of your promise to keep your brain strong and healthy!

MY STRONG BRAIN PLEDGE

for

_____

I pledge to keep my brain strong and healthy.
I will learn more about what my brain does.
I will make good choices and protect my brain as
it grows and develops.

I will practice naming and understanding all my feelings by:

☐ Learning the names of my feelings!

☐ Deciding what my body needs or wants
when I have a feeling!

☐ Ask for help when I don't know the name of a feeling.

A Note from the Author

The Know Your Neuro series is designed to do two things:

1) Teach kids about their brain so that they will want to protect it and keep it strong.

2) Grow executive function skills.

Parents can do this too! Remember, risky behavior arrests healthy brain development and can slow down skill growth. For more resources, use the videos and handouts in

KnowYourNeuro.org

to be a Brain-Savvy Parent and Caregiver!

Crystal Collier, PhD, LPC-S

Follow MORE of Neuro's Adventures in:

Know Your Neuro!
Neuro Makes Good Choices
Neuro Sets Boundaries
Neuro Says No!
Neuro Learns Self-Control
Neuro Grows Positive Self-Talk
Neuro Accepts Their Body
Neuro Grows Sharing Skills
Neuro Asks for Help

Made in the USA
Coppell, TX
25 November 2024

40956668R00024